On Location

A comedy

Stephen Smith

Samuel French—London
New York-Toronto-Hollywood

FOR AMATEUR PRODUCTION ENQUIRIES

UNITED KINGDOM AND WORLD
EXCLUDING NORTH AMERICA
plays@samuelfrench.co.uk
020 7255 4302/01

Each title is subject to availability from Samuel French,
depending upon country of performance.

ON LOCATION

First performed by WCP at Waterbeach School, Cambridge-shire, on 15th November 2000, as the second half of a double bill with *Background Artiste*, with the following cast of characters:

Malcolm	Bill Bullivant
Mary	Jane Stewart
Roddy	Garry Fowler
Sam	Christine Gilsenan
Victoria	Valmai Furness
Background Artistes	Martin Andrus, Roy Furness, Michael Williamson

Produced and directed by Stephen Smith
Designed by Mark Easterfield
Stage managed by Julie Petrucci

CHARACTERS

Malcolm, middle-aged
Mary, 30s
Roddy, middle-aged
Sam, third assistant director, young
Victoria, elderly
Extras

The action takes place in a church hall

Time—the present

Other plays by Stephen Smith
published by Samuel French Ltd

Background Artiste
Departure
One-sided Triangle
Parentcraft

ON LOCATION

A church hall in London. Winter, 6.30 a.m.

The hall is being used as the canteen of a film crew on location. Centrally, at the rear of the hall, is a pair of double doors through which all entrances and exits are made. On the L wall there is a display of children's paintings and on the R wall is a notice-board with various church notices and local events. R of the doors are several children's toys scattered about and L is a large table. UR is a smaller table with two chairs. UL is another table with two chairs. A bottle of tomato ketchup stands on the table

When the CURTAIN rises, several of the film crew (i.e. real "background artistes") are sitting at the larger table R of the doors drinking tea and reading newspapers. Malcolm, a fairly scruffily dressed middle-aged man, sits at the table UR eating a cooked breakfast. On the floor beside him is a supermarket carrier containing a paperback

After a few seconds Mary, a smartly dressed woman, timidly enters and, on seeing Malcolm on his own, walks up to him. She carries a piece of paper

Mary Excuse me, (*looking at the piece of paper*) could you tell me where I could find Sam McNabb, please.

Malcolm (*without looking up*) In bed most likely.

Mary (*surprised*) Pardon?

Malcolm (*vaguely pointing in the direction from which she's come*) Grab yourself something to eat first.

Mary (*after a pause*) You see I was told to report to him at six thirty.

Malcolm Her.

Mary What?

Malcolm Sam's a her. Samantha.

Mary Oh.

Malcolm She'll come here looking for you, so go and grab something to eat.

Mary I've already eaten.

Malcolm That was stupid then, wasn't it. Got to get as much out of this lot as you can. They'll screw you otherwise. (*He looks at Mary*) Financially speaking that is. A hot meal every five and half hours is what we're entitled to. Stop taking them and it won't be long before we stop getting them. Not much left in our favour so we've got to make a stand in the food.

Mary Suppose I didn't really know what the food would be like.

Malcolm Snob are you?

Mary (*shocked*) No!

Malcolm All snouts in the same trough here. May have to wait for the cast and crew but we all get the same grub.

Mary (*looking at his plate*) Good is it?

Malcolm Not bad.

Mary Anyway I stayed in a Bed and Breakfast so I had already paid …

Malcolm Bed and Breakfast! You're not going to be making very much out of today are you?

Mary Too early for a train, I get lost driving in London, so I thought best to come up the night before. Had its advantages, didn't have to get up until five thirty, if I'd driven from Bournemouth ——

Malcolm Bournemouth!

Mary Yes.

Malcolm Definitely not be making anything out of this game. Don't get expenses you know.

Mary Yes I know.

Malcolm Not a glory seeker are you?

Mary (*annoyed*) This Sam McNab, what do you mean she'd still be in bed?

Malcolm Probably up now.

Mary Does she live near here?

Malcolm See all the trucks parked along the road outside. She lives in one of them on location. The Winnebago next to the honeywagon.

Mary The what?

Malcolm The camper next to the bogs.

Mary Oh ... right ... well, perhaps I'd better find her.

Malcolm Up to you.

Mary Right. (*She starts to exit and then comes back*) Er — if she does come while I'm away my name's Cavendish. Mary Cavendish.

Malcolm nods

And you are?

Malcolm Still eating.

Mary Right.

Mary exits

Malcolm continues eating

Roddy enters balancing his breakfast tray and carrying a large holdall at the same time. Roddy is about the same age as Malcolm but wears much brighter clothes. He looks around and then heads straight to Malcolm

Roddy Malc, mind if I join you?

Roddy puts down his tray before Malcolm has a chance to answer. He puts his holdall on the chair while he unpacks it and, during the following, proceeds to take out all sorts of vitamin pills, bottled water, his own glass and cleaning equipment

Malcolm Do I have any choice?

Roddy Don't be like that, love.

Malcolm Howard with you?

Roddy Take more money than this to get that old cow out of bed these days.

Malcolm We're not good enough for him now, are we?

Roddy Not since he landed that bloody presenter's job on satellite.

Malcolm Pays well?

Roddy Four-fifty a day and all the frocks he wants. Makes me feel like Cinderella's frog.

Malcolm Life's one big fairy story for you, isn't it?

Roddy No it isn't. Not with Howard boasting he can have as many slots as he likes. Made me feel very insecure. But I plucked up courage and said, in my most sternest voice: "Howard, if you forget your roots you won't stay blonde for long" and gave him one of my severe looks.

Malcolm Without Howard, I expect we're going to be surrounded by wide-eyed amateurs again.

Roddy Alf's got no-one left. *Casualty*'s Christmas Day special has cleaned him out. Apparently a plane, carrying the EU endangered species committee, crashes into a load of trainspotters and then flips on to the World Morris Dancing Championships. Bells and notebooks are strewn everywhere.

Malcolm Why aren't you doing it then?

Roddy Don't do anything with blood in it. Gives me the willies, in the metaphorical sense that is. Won't do war films, hospital dramas and *Brookside*. Why aren't you doing it?

Malcolm I hate Bristol.

Roddy *(cleaning his glass)* Not *Casualty*'s fault it's shot in Bristol.

Malcolm Come to think of it, I hate the whole West Country. In fact I hate anything that is West. East Anglia, East Midlands even the North-East I can live with, but I hate the West with a passion. That's how I grew to love Eastern Europe and detest West Ham. Where were you born?

Roddy East Grinstead.

Malcolm Knew it. That's why I'm prepared to put up with you. Despite your deviant behaviour.

Roddy Speaking of deviants, his majesty wouldn't have been able to come today even if he wanted to. Gonna have to present from a prone position for the next few weeks.

Malcolm Do what?

Roddy On the show. Stupid bitch twisted her ankle spring cleaning. Our feather duster can be uncontrollable at the best of times. Got a mind of it's own. The amount of times I've said, "It's too big even for you, Howard, stick to the J Cloth", but he never listens. (*He puts the holdall on the floor*)

Malcolm I know the feeling.

Roddy (*cleaning his seat*) At least it's stopped him buying that motorbike. I quite like the leathers but I'm too old to be clinging to someone's back with a great big throbbing thing between my legs. (*Sitting down and looking at his plate*) Are your sausages small?

Malcolm No.

Roddy Look at mine. Bloody pig these came from must have been anorexic.

Malcolm (*reaching for them*) I'll have 'em if you don't want them.

Roddy Bet these baked beans came out of one of those five p cans, it's like a couple of islands in a vast orange sea.

Malcolm Get some more then.

Roddy Can't. Bloody caterer's got it in for me. Ever since I accused him of having an affair with Howard, I get small portions. Story of my life, I suppose.

Malcolm Story of your life is accusing everyone of having an affair with Howard.

Roddy Who's the third A.D.?

Malcolm Sam.

Roddy Oh wonderful, that's all I need, little Miss Bountiful.

Malcolm What's wrong with Sam, she's all right.

Roddy It's that so-called actor she hangs around with, Dirk the jerk.

Malcolm Dirk van Dyke.

Roddy What sort of name is that, Dirk van Dyke, sounds like a lesbian lorry driver.

Malcolm Sam obviously doesn't think so.

Roddy And who wears the trousers in that relationship I ask myself, she's got a man's name and he's always preening himself.

Malcolm You're a fine one to talk.

Roddy Sorry, but being splashed at a bus stop doesn't constitute being an actor in my book. I'm still not convinced it's his torso in that shower ad. A head like his on a body like that's unnatural.

Malcolm Have you got a crush on him or something?

Roddy (*getting tomato ketchup from the other table*) Not me, love, I have my standards.

Malcolm Then who?

Roddy Seems to spend more time stacking shelves at Tesco's than acting. Saw him the other day manhandling some grapefruits, I shouted out, "Is that what you call product placement, Dirk?" Didn't see the funny side.

Malcolm Howard's got a crush on him, hasn't he?

Roddy More crumble than crush. The sight of Dirk literally makes him go weak at the knees. If that shower advert is on while Howard's ironing he becomes a fire hazard. I told him how could he fall for some actor who spends most of his life sitting at a checkout. He had no answer to that. Flounced off in a huff with the feather duster.

Malcolm Dangerous to spring clean in a huff.

Roddy Few minutes later I hear a scream and discover him spread-eagled in the kitchen covered in mango chutney. He'd tried to reach a crevice that needs someone to support the stepladder and brought all the condiments down on himself. Is that Freudian or what.

Sam enters. She is the third assistant director, in her early twenties. She is wearing very casual clothes and a headset and carries a clipboard. Victoria, an elderly and very elegantly dressed lady who carries a large handbag, follows her

Sam All ready for action, chaps? (*She looks at her clipboard and then looks around*) Oh dear, one missing.

Malcolm Gone looking for you.

Sam Why didn't you tell her to wait here?

Malcolm I did.

Sam Anyway, let's tick you off. (*Doing so on her clipboard*) Malcolm, Roddy, and which one are you? Mary or Victoria?

Roddy Of bridges?

Victoria Suspension mainly but a good cantilever can bring a tear
    to the eye.

Roddy You can say that again.

Victoria (*going to look at the children's drawings on the wall*)
    Every month we pick one out of the atlas to visit. Been all over the
    world, unfortunately we've still to do Hull.

Sam enters with Mary

Sam Found our lost sheep.

Roddy Lamb.

Sam Pardon?

Roddy Didn't Mary have a little lamb?

Victoria (*laughing*) Oh very good, Roderick.

Roddy Roddy please. I'm not the rat from *Tales of the Riverbank*.

Malcolm No, more a weasel from *Wind in the Willows*.

Sam (*ignoring him*) Good to see we have a happy bunch here today.
    Now, here's your form, Mary, (*handing her the form*) and don't
    go running off again, please. Fill this in and get Phil, the second
    A.D., to sign it before you go.

Mary How will I find him?

Sam You'll meet him on set. I'll just go and see what the situation
    is with make-up and wardrobe.

Sam exits

Victoria (*excited*) Are we going to be made-up? How spiffing. I
    usually do my own.

Malcolm As a mutant?

Victoria Is that what we are?

Malcolm Do you hire someone to do your thinking for you?

Victoria Life's an adventure to be lived. If you know what's around
    the next corner, might as well stay at home.

Malcolm Some of us can't afford the luxury of staying at home.

Victoria My father always used to say imagination and excitement
    cost nothing.

Roddy That's so true, the most exciting times with Howard have been when we use our imagination.

Victoria Inhabitants of some fictional eastern European country are they?

Malcolm Roddy and Howard?

Victoria No, these Mutants. Imagine they come from somewhere called Mutania.

Mary Have you never seen *Star Trek*?

Victoria Sorry, don't watch television.

Mary Never?

Victoria Prefer a good book, or a good man or a good horse. Not necessarily in that order. Depends on the light.

Roddy What about films?

Victoria Not really a cinemagoer. Find the screens too big. Nothing I want to see that's bigger than life size. Not with an audience anyhow.

Roddy Missed one of life's uplifting experiences.

Malcolm Marilyn Monroe.

Roddy I was thinking more of the *African Queen*.

Victoria Always a disappointment, I feel. Prefer to participate. Why watch someone hanging off a bridge when you can do it yourself.

Malcolm My thought exactly.

Mary Then what are you doing here?

Victoria Participating. Curiosity's my middle name, should've been a cat. Actually I shouldn't, our cat drowned when I tried to baptize it after a rather awe-inspiring church service at age five.

Malcolm Pity it wasn't the other way round.

Victoria To be completely honest my middle name's really Matilda. Do apologize, totally incorrect statement to have made. Don't know what came over me. Must be the thrill of filming.

Roddy The roar of the director and the smell of the frocks.

Victoria Precisely. How poetic.

Malcolm How pathetic.

Mary (*going and sitting at the large table* L) Yes ... well ... I'd better fill my form in.

Victoria Am I expected to?

Roddy Why not, it's participating.

Victoria So it is.

Mary (*searching her handbag*) Excuse me, has anyone got a pen?

Victoria Certainly, me dear. (*She produces an expensive pen from her large handbag which she hands to Mary*)

Mary Thank you. (*She starts filling in her form*)

Victoria (*searching in her bag*) Oh drat, seem to have mislaid my reading glasses.

Mary I'll fill yours in for you if you'd like.

Victoria How kind. (*She gives Mary the form and stands next to her*)

Mary Name?

Victoria Henrietta Matilda Victoria Frobisher.

Mary Sorry?

Victoria Rather a mouthful I'm afraid.

Roddy Just put down Posh Spice.

Victoria And what sort of spice would that be?

Malcolm Dill.

Mary Why so many names?

Victoria After relatives. Father wanted a boy. Henry Matthew Victor. All my clothes were monogrammed before I was born. HMV.

Mary I see.

Victoria Had a thing about dogs and gramophones but we don't talk about it. I ended up with the female versions.

Roddy And became Her Mistress's Voice.

Victoria Became all sorts of things. At school I got called His Majesty's Vehicle.

Roddy That's class for you. So much better than being called an old bike.

Mary But you prefer Victoria.

Victoria Sums me up better than Henrietta which is Teutonic for ruler of the home. Not exactly me, as I'm never there, whereas Victoria means victorious.

Mary What about Matilda?

Victoria Sounds like a pantomime cow. (*Rummaging in her bag*) Does anyone mind if I smoke?

Malcolm Yes.
Victoria (*shocked*) Oh … people don't usually say yes.
Malcolm Which is why polluters like you get away with it.
Victoria Sorry. I'll just nip outside for a quick one then.

Victoria exits

Mary Don't have to be so rude to her.
Malcolm Why?
Mary It's not nice for the rest of us.

Sam enters and tells the extras on the US table they are needed. They all exit during the following, leaving one newspaper behind

Malcolm Neither's smoking …
Sam (*looking around*) Right, wardrobe and make-up are ready so let's start with — er — Malcolm. Don't need to tell you where to go, do I?
Malcolm No.

Malcolm gets up and exits

Sam Only one stylist and make-up artist so best to go individually.
Roddy When are they going to use us?
Sam Not sure at present.
Mary But it's a spoof sci-fi film?
Sam Sort of.
Roddy Why not remove the "s" and make it a poof sci-fi for a change. Lots of my friends would be up for a remake of *Flash Gordon*.
Sam No, sorry, Roddy.
Roddy One can but dream.
Mary "Star Trek the Next Generation Game"?
Sam What?
Mary My agent said that I was a mutant in "Star Trek the Next Generation Game".

Sam That was just a British working title the producers punted around for a while to stir up interest. Don't believe everything your agent tells you.

Roddy Don't believe anything anyone tells you in this business. The producers tell the investors all sorts of superstars will appear until the investors cough up. By a quirk of fate it's always a day too late to sign said superstars, but never mind we have an unknown, on the verge of the greatness, to save the day. Translated, this is some no-hoper who came free with a packet of Coco-pops. (*To Sam*) Is Dirk in it?

Sam (*annoyed*) Yes, he's playing the lead.

Roddy Who's playing the dog.

Sam Very funny. Do you want to work today, Roddy?

Victoria enters a little unsteadily

Victoria (*sitting next to Roddy*) Hope I haven't missed anything. Just had to go outside for a quick puff.

Mary Was there an American working title then?

Sam "FT".

Mary Which was short for?

Sam "ET 2".

Mary "ET 2"?

Sam "ET" as in "Extra Terrestrial". "2" as in sequel. You know how the Americans love to put the English language into a food processor.

Mary So "FT" could be "Final Terrestrial".

Victoria Or Fat Testicle. (*Realizing what she's said*) Sorry.

Roddy Therefore the prequel would be "DT — Drunken Terrestrial". Don't phone home, phone for a cab.

Mary What's the new title?

Sam "Star Chores, or the Confessions of an Intergalactic Dustman".

Mary (*shocked*) A sex film?

Sam Not exactly.

Victoria (*excitedly, going to Sam*) Do we have to take our clothes off?

Sam No.

Victoria Pity, always had an ambition to run naked up a drawbridge under a full moon.

Roddy Thank God no producer's had an ambition to film it.

Victoria Quite a stunner when I was younger, I'll have you know. Oh well, *que sera sera,* might as well get a cup of tea, as my nanny used to say.

Victoria exits

Sam Sure it's cigarettes she's smoking?

Mary No.

Roddy What's the treatment then?

Mary Isn't she too old for anything now?

Sam (*sitting next to Mary*) He means the film storyline.

Mary (*embarrassed*) Oh.

Sam It's about the adventures of a space refuse collector chasing a rogue meteor. The writers thought instead of a meteor crashing into Earth, why not turn the concept on its head and have a man chasing a meteor.

Roddy Butch is he?

Sam You know what Dirk looks like.

Roddy No, I meant the rogue meteor.

Sam Solid as a rock.

Roddy Sounds just my kind of movie. Camp without the tents.

Mary And what are we?

Sam Still mutants. No matter what story line they decide on we still need mutants. However the budget's tight, so make-up and wardrobe have to improvise. Still that's what makes life interesting. Doesn't it, Roddy?

Sam exits

Roddy One advantage if loverboy is playing the lead, we won't have to buy a cinema ticket. (*Putting the plates together*) It'll go straight to video.

Mary Not very famous then?

Roddy I believe he played a Thesaurus in *Jurassic Park.*

Mary You don't seem to like him very much.

Roddy Dirk Van Dyke thinks he's God's gift to the human race and no-one seems to see through it. (*He takes the plates to the extras' table* us)

Mary My agent called him his matinée idol.

Roddy (*sitting next to Mary*) Idle as in bone bloody idle would be about right.

Mary I see. (*Pause*) Is it always like this?

Roddy On jobs from Alf it is. He gets all the cheap TV and movies who need to cut a deal. This your first call?

Mary Yes. I saw the Alfredo Leache Artistes advert in the *Stage* and while I was at the interview he offered me this. Said I didn't need to pay to go into the directory until I found out what it's like.

Roddy Yes, well, he's rather stretched at the moment, everyone's in *Casualty*.

Mary Lot of flu about. You've done a lot of this, have you?

Roddy Do anything me. Cabaret at weekends and couple of these a week to keep the bitches from the door.

Mary Alf gives you a couple of jobs a week?

Roddy No, only when he's looking for money for the next directory. Wouldn't trust him further than I can throw him. No, I'm with several agencies for Extras work and I've got an agent for my cabaret stuff.

Mary Which is?

Roddy Country and Western Drag at pubs and clubs with my partner Howard. He plays his organ and I strut my stuff. In Hackney they haven't realized Tammy Wynette is dead; think she's just fallen on hard times. Not a bad living unless the van breaks down on the way to Swansea. Howard earns a lot more than me. Put him in front of a camera and he becomes Carol Vorderman. Works for one of these satellite stations, UK Just About Breathing or something. Gets paid to talk to people about hanging wallpaper, hanging baskets and hanging around street corners.

Mary In one programme?

Roddy No, loads of different ones. Does five shows a day back to back three days a week. One day he did DIY, pruning your privets, transsexuals, dress designing and car maintenance. He said each show seemed to flow into the next.

Victoria enters with two cups of coffee

Victoria Malcolm's not a very jolly person, is he?

Roddy Won't be doing adverts for breakfast cereals that's for sure.

Victoria I saw him standing outside the costumes van. I waved but he totally ignored me.

Mary Certainly very rude, I'm surprised nobody's told him where to go.

Victoria (*standing between Roddy and Mary*) Personally, I wouldn't know where to send him.

Roddy Don't worry, he's like that with everyone.

Mary Known him long?

Roddy Met him in the clubs when I first started out in the seventies. Stand-up comic, would you believe.

Mary Black comedy, was it?

Roddy Sort of reddy green, definitely not blue.

Victoria Puce.

Roddy Could say that. Instead of thrilling leftwing intellectuals where he could've made a packet, deliberately played all the wrong venues. Little personal crusade to relieve his beloved working-class of mother-in-law jokes. Problem was in those days all PC meant was a packet of condoms.

Victoria Yes, not many people had computers.

Roddy Struggled on for years until his mother died. Once her encouragement had gone he finally threw in the towel. Too late. Thrown it in earlier, he'd have another career by now. Never get anywhere without timing.

Mary When was this?

Roddy Years ago. Got an Equity card but prefers to do this sort of thing. No pressure and all the moaning he wants. In a perverse sort of way he's funnier now than he was on stage. But it's not the sort of humour that wins friends and influences people.

Sam enters

Sam Right, Roddy, you can go to make-up now.

Roddy Quick detour first. (*Going to the table, opening his bag and with one movement sweeping his stuff into it while singing*) "*Que sera sera.*" Might as well go for a pee. As my grandad used to say. (*He winks at Victoria*)

Roddy exits

Victoria (*sitting next to Mary*) Not very far behind Malcolm in the rude stakes and not very trusting.

Sam But very wise. Anyone could wander in here so keep your valuables with you at all times.

Mary What's happening at the moment?

Sam We're shooting a scene across the road in the adventure playground.

Victoria How thrilling.

Sam Our hero has captured the rogue meteor but while loading knocked out his navigation system and crash landed on to the planet West Acton in Zone 3. He must now make his way back on the perilous interplanetary central line to his faraway home planet of Redbridge.

Mary And where do we come in?

Sam Mile End.

Victoria That sounds a ghastly place.

Sam It is.

Mary Doing what?

Sam Coming out of the bushes near the public toilets.

Victoria Gosh how exciting, reminds me of my youth.

Sam What's in those cigarettes you smoke?

Victoria Very healthy. No nicotine, strictly herbal.

Sam Friend gave them to you?

Victoria As a matter of fact, yes, in the Hindu Kush.

Sam What, that takeaway in Bethnal Green?

Victoria No, the mountain range in Pakistan. Surprisingly refreshing. Makes one feel jolly and light-headed. Like one?

Sam Not while I'm working. Perhaps at the wrap.

Victoria Meet you there then. Always enjoy going to new places.

Sam Yes ... right ... well, must get back to the action.

Mary How long do you think it'll be to our scene?

Sam Couple of hours. We've still got to paint the climbing frame for our hero's entrance into the White City.

Sam exits

Victoria Just us two now then.

Mary Yes like the nursery rhyme.

Victoria Pardon.

Mary About the green bottles hanging on the wall. You know, (*singing*) "If one green bottle should accidentally fall ..."

Victoria I hope not. I've got an artificial hip.

Mary I wasn't being serious.

Victoria Oh good. (*She gets up and looks around*) Ingenious, these film people. Very clever use of an adventure playground.

Mary Sounds a very cheap way of making a film.

Victoria Amazingly expensive to make. This one is costing millions.

Mary Of what, pesetas?

Victoria No, pounds.

Mary How do you know?

Victoria Because my bridge club have invested in it.

Mary Your bridge club?

Victoria Yes, we travel the world admiring the architecture of bridges. Surprising how much bridges and films have in common. Suspension bridges and suspension of disbelief. As investors, part of our dividend is a chance to appear in the film.

Mary So you're all angels.

Victoria I wouldn't exactly say that. Cynthia's been done for shoplifting at Iceland. Although it was a very hot day and had simply forgotten the frozen leg of pork temporarily placed down her vest to cool down. Sort of mistake anyone could have made.

Mary No, angels are people who invest in films.

Victoria (*laughing*) To balance out all the devils that make them I should imagine.

Mary Possibly so.

Victoria I'm the first to venture forth so to speak. Lead the charge and report back is my mission.

Mary How many of you are there?

Victoria Thirty-seven. Well thirty-seven at dawn this morning. May have lost one during the day, never know.

Mary Are the rest all like you?

Victoria No, God forbid. (*Walking up to Mary*) Some of them are slightly eccentric.

Mary So how did you come to invest in this film?

Victoria Jolly interesting story actually. We were admiring the segmented arches of the Ponte Vecchio in Florence. That's Florence the Italian city not Florence Wilberforce our Treasurer. Have you seen them?

Mary What?

Victoria Florence's segmented arches.

Mary No.

Victoria Fifteen twenty-seven.

Mary That was when it was built?

Victoria No, it was the time the coach was to pick up. Anyway it was late because of a puncture and whilst we were waiting for its repair, some film chappies passed by.

Mary How did you know they were "film chappies"?

Victoria Because they were carrying one of those huge furry gerbils on a pole. Ascertained the producer's name was Jeremy and he'd been working on a film for several years, that would be a surefire winner, but had only raised half the money, so we voluntered to help finance the project.

Mary How much?

Victoria Not sure exactly as when we got back he visited us individually. I only put in ten thousand pounds because I'm having an extension put on to the west wing.

Mary So your bridge club could be financing the whole film?

Victoria Oh no. Jeremy told us he was matching all our funding. However, as our interest, we did stipulate that it had to feature a decent bridge. That must be why the storyline ends at this planet Redbridge.

Sam enters

Sam Don't eat your vegetables and you too could look like this.

Malcolm enters dressed as a sort of badly designed swamp creature. He is all in green with green and red make-up and yellow rubber gloves

Malcolm Very funny. (*Unhappily, he goes to sit on his chair*)
Sam (*looking at her clipboard*) OK Victoria, you're next.
Victoria (*looking at Malcolm*) How spiffing, am I going to look like this?
Sam That's up to the stylist. Do you know where to go?
Malcolm (*getting out his paperback from his bag under the chair*) I could tell her.
Victoria No need, I'm ready to zoom in for a wild-track.

Victoria exits excitedly

Sam What's the matter with Roddy? He's been making snide comments about Dirk all morning.
Malcolm No idea what goes on in Roddy's head. It's a magical mystery tour.
Sam Must have some idea.
Malcolm He suspects Dirk likes meat and two veg as well as quiche.
Sam What?
Malcolm Since Howard's landed this new job Roddy's gone warp factor five into insecure mode. Reckons everyone's after Howard now.
Sam (*laughing*) Dirk and Howard.
Malcolm That's Roddy for you.
Sam When will he get it into his thick skull that not all men are like him.
Malcolm Or like Howard.
Sam (*suddenly worried*) There isn't any truth in it, is there?
Malcolm How should I know, he's your boyfriend.

Sam I hate this business.

Sam exits

Mary Speaking of personal vendettas, what have you got against Victoria? She's invested ten grand in this film.

Malcolm This is why we get paid a pittance. Too many toffs with more money than sense reeking havoc everywhere they go as usual.

Mary (*going to him*) Sorry, but it's difficult to take you seriously in that outfit.

Malcolm Just my point. This is all a game to the likes of you and her ladyship. You flounce in with no experience, no training and get paid the same as us.

Mary Isn't the point supposed to be that we don't need any. If it worries you so much, why not do something you've been trained to do?

Malcolm Like what?

Mary Go back to being a stand-up comic again.

Malcolm Who told you about that?

Mary Roddy.

Malcolm That bitch can't keep her trap shut, can she.

Mary (*sitting next to him*) He was just explaining why you are like this.

Malcolm Like what?

Mary A bloody pain in the neck.

Malcolm I'm a bloody pain in the neck, am I?

Mary Seem to take great delight in upsetting as many people as possible. Are you smiling under all that?

Malcolm A little. Not a lot to smile about these days.

Mary You're not the only person with problems, you know. I thought I was leading a perfectly happy life until I found out my husband had been screwing around ever since we've been married.

Malcolm So you're on your own too?

Mary For the first time in ten years. I've had to start my life again so no reason why you can't.

Malcolm The difference is I'm the result of my own downfall you're not. Correction: it wasn't even a downfall, I'd never reached any peak high enough to fall down from.

Mary Can't be that bad.

Malcolm A comedian who doesn't make the punters laugh is a failure, pure and simple.

Mary Find something else then.

Malcolm I thought I had.

Mary Why not do what Roddy does and perform at weekends.

Malcolm Dressed as a woman!

Mary No, something that can benefit from your comic background.

Malcolm Wouldn't hold Roddy up as an example of someone who's cracked it. He always ends up clinging to the coat-tails of another man until he eventually loses his grip. Howard's but one in a long line. Been together a couple of years and he's already jealous of his success.

Mary Perhaps this time will be different.

Malcolm I doubt it. Roddy's not got what it takes to make it on his own in this business but he's very good at pushing his partners in the right direction and living off them for a few years. Made himself a professional stepping-stone and then wonders why the tide always washes over him.

Roddy makes a grand entrance wearing a bizarre pink costume with a blonde wig

Roddy How do I look?

Malcolm Unique.

Roddy Princess Tammy from the planet Randomly Dressed.

Mary Do we all have to decide on our character?

Malcolm Only obligatory if your name begins with an "r".

Roddy (*in an American accent*) Formerly known as Miss Mississipi Mutant, I reached number thirty-nine with the chip fryer's anthem "Stand By Your Pan", a sorry little tale about a couple of King Edwards and a cod. Both end up battered in the stomach of a welder from Aberystwyth.

Malcolm Not the act here, please Roddy, I've heard it a thousand times.

Roddy How can you, I haven't done it a thousand times.

Mary What's a welder from Aberystwyth doing in Mississippi?

Roddy Now there hangs a tale.

Malcolm And a few pints before it's funny.

Roddy Worked with the darling Virgina Pugh, you know.

Mary Who?

Malcolm Tammy Wynette.

Mary Singing?

Roddy On a daytime soap in the States called "Capital" in 1987.

Malcolm *Maître d'* who showed her to her table and called for the wine waiter.

Roddy Always been able to carry myself well.

Malcolm Had to sleep with the producer to get that part.

Roddy All the under-fives had to sleep with the producer. Perk of the job.

Malcolm Under-fives lines, not years by the way.

Roddy First rung above extra in the States. Double the money and another twenty-five dollars for wearing my own tux.

Mary You worked in America?

Roddy Reasonably attractive when I was younger, would you believe. I was the original Cigarillo man.

Malcolm You were the only Cigarillo man.

Roddy My face was plastered all over London.

Malcolm But you should have seen the other guy.

Mary Who was Cigarillo man?

Roddy More sophisticated than Marlboro man.

Malcolm He didn't ride a horse he took a taxi.

Mary I've never heard of cigarillos.

Malcolm Is it surprising, one look at Roddy poncing around with a big hat and a small cigar is enough to kill any advertising campaign.

Roddy Made my name as a male model though; it wasn't long before I was swanning around swimming pools doing my Rock Hudson routine.

Malcolm With his cigarillos.

Roddy Don't knock them, the adverts were shown all over the world. I was really big in Mozambique, I got mobbed in Maputo.

Mary What happened then?

Roddy They got my wristwatch, wallet, cuff links and matches. The only thing I had left was my cigarillos.

Mary No, I meant what happened to your career?

Roddy Cosmetic surgery.

Mary You had cosmetic surgery?

Roddy No, I didn't. If I had, it would be me advertising the latest bonkotronic on satellite instead of Howard.

Malcolm Scared of the knife. Wouldn't even play a surgeon in *General Hospital.*

Roddy When the competition are five years older but look younger and thinner then it's time to go home. No worse place than the States to be a loser.

Mary You don't seem that bad to me.

Roddy Thank you, kind lady, but at my age, even in this country, professionally speaking, I make a better woman than a man.

Mary That's very sad.

Malcolm It is for women.

Roddy (*sprawling himself on the table*) That's show business, ducky.

Malcolm From a swan to a duck.

Roddy Or a fag to a drag.

Sam enters

Sam Have you seen that Victoria woman?

Malcolm As opposed to the Victoria man?

Sam You know what I mean.

Mary Isn't she in make-up?

Sam She was, she's gone missing. I hope she hasn't been smoking those cigarettes again and ended up in a pond.

Malcolm Is that any great loss?

Sam We can't afford to have her wandering about.

Roddy Hardly a top secret film.

Sam That's not the point. (*She starts to exit*)
Mary (*running up to Sam*) Do you want me next?
Sam Not until I've found Victoria, it was my job to keep tabs on the
old bag.

Sam hurriedly exits

*Mary forlornly looks around and eventually starts reading the
newspaper left on the extras' table* US

Roddy Unlike Sam to get her knickers in a knot over a missing
extra. Lot on her mind I expect. What with Romeo-boy looking
for any opening he can find.
Malcolm Have you got any proof about Howard and Dirk?
Roddy Found a bottle of that shampoo he advertises yesterday.
Malcolm I've got a Barclaycard but I haven't been to bed with
Rowan Atkinson.
Roddy I have more conclusive proof than that. Didn't appear on
Poirot for nothing you know.
Malcolm No, you appeared for sixty-five quid the same as the rest
of us.
Roddy If you don't want to hear it then I won't tell you.
Malcolm Up to you.
Roddy (*leaping off the table and sitting next to Malcolm*) All right
you've twisted my arm. The other day Howard was having a very
secretive phone-call.
Malcolm How do you know it was secretive?
Roddy He was using his conspiratorial whisper. As soon as he left
I pressed call return and who should answer the phone. Dirk the
jerk. I rest my case.
Malcolm Sure it was him?
Roddy Course I am. I'd recognize that fake Shakespearian whine
at twenty paces. Howard has set his eyes on Dirk and what
Howard wants Howard gets.
Malcolm And Dirk has no say in it at all has he?
Roddy The only thoughts Dirk has are written on the autocue.

Mary (*looking up from her paper*) Perhaps Sam is afraid Victoria's going to find out where her ten grand has gone.

Roddy What ten grand?

Mary Victoria has invested in this film. And all her mates have too.

Roddy How much?

Mary A lot.

Roddy Well, with the lot on this film she'll certainly never see it again.

Victoria enters in a posh frock

Victoria They wanted me to be a dung beetle but I was having none of that.

Malcolm Been there dung that.

Victoria I'd never live it down.

Mary So what are you?

Victoria Grand Duchess Anastasia. The youngest daughter of Tsar Nicholas II.

Mary In a sci-fi film?

Victoria Great mystery surrounds her. She was believed to have been executed in 1918 but various people have since claimed to be her.

Malcolm When you get past eighty you start claiming to be whoever you last saw on telly.

Victoria Perhaps she was whisked away to a faraway planet.

Mary Like Elvis Presley.

Roddy They could be presenting the Elvis and Anastasia show on Uranus. I'd certainly watch it. (*He gets a camping magazine out of his bag to read*)

Victoria See what a little imagination can do, Malcolm.

Malcolm I've never disputed you've got a little imagination, Victoria.

Sam enters

Sam Ah, found you, Victoria. Thought you got lost.

Victoria No, I was just on a little recce.

Sam A little recce?

Victoria For the bridge club. See how the investment is being spent.

Sam Ah, well, I'm only the third assistant director. I just deal with the extras.

Roddy Background artistes!

Sam Background artistes. I don't have anything to do with the finances.

Victoria I know that, my dear.

Sam You do. Oh good.

Victoria And a fine job you do too, running around looking after us.

Sam Thank you. (*She starts to exit*)

Mary (*running up to Sam*) Shall I go now?

Sam No, not yet, I have something to attend to first.

Sam exits

Malcolm Got Sam worried. Gone running back to sir.

Victoria Why?

Malcolm She thinks you'll withdraw the funding if you discover the truth.

Victoria What truth is that?

Malcolm Far be it from me to tell you, but can't you see what a third-rate film this is.

Mary (*sitting down*) What are you going to do?

Victoria Make sure the money is spent on the film and not the producer.

Mary How will you do that?

Victoria With my eyes. (*Getting out her notebook*) So far I've counted one costume wagon, one make-up wagon, one honey-wagon, three Winnebagos and a catering wagon.

Roddy Perhaps this is the *Generation Game* after all.

Victoria Norma Falconbridge's daughter Tango is in the film business and reckons if I give her all the details she can estimate the spend.

Roddy Tango?

Victoria Her father, Wing Commander Falconbridge, never used christian names in the RAF so he called his children Bravo, Echo, Tango and Foxtrot.

Mary What was Foxtrot?

Victoria A very unhappy boy. But Tango's done well for herself and knows the film business inside out. She's discovered Jeremy has a reputation for conning investors into making low budget movies then selling them for a pittance to his own distribution company.

Mary Why are you still doing it then?

Victoria Tango suggested we use the Enterprise Investment Scheme to gain tax relief and shelter from capital gains. She also put a clause in the contract which releases the film to majority investors in case of a dispute.

Malcolm And you intend to set up your own distribution company?

Victoria Good God no. That would be far too much trouble.

Malcolm How else is it going to get seen?

Victoria Only by a select few. With all the famous wealthy extras in the film we'll easily recoup our investment with strictly limited showings. Friends and family will pay handsomely to see us all make fools of ourselves.

Roddy So this will be a film where the audience comes to watch the extras not the actors.

Victoria Exactly.

Roddy And Dirk thinks this is his big breakthrough! I feel better already.

Victoria Of course we want it to be as good as possible. Everyone is getting paid, no-one will be out of pocket. Except Jeremy of course.

Roddy As a leading extra, if you ever want me to attend some of these special screenings …

Victoria We might take you up on that.

Roddy I also do a great cabaret turn with my partner Howard called "Two Lonely Soles in Search of their Shoes". Very contemporary with a slice of the past and a dollop of a mascara.

Victoria Perhaps that as well.

Mary I don't think I'm cut out for this extras lark. Too much back-biting.

Roddy Malcolm's OK once you've done some filming. Then you're one of the oppressed.

Mary Too much sitting around.

Roddy Now that is a skill he's perfected to a fine art.

Mary Too much uncertainty.

Victoria You like your life organized.

Mary I thought I'd like the excitement of the unknown but found out I don't.

Victoria And you are good at organizing other lives.

Mary I like to help.

Victoria How about working for us?

Mary Your bridge club?

Victoria Why not.

Mary Do they really exist?

Victoria Of course. We are bunch of rich lonely ladies in search of excitement but other people's excitement takes a lot of organiz-ing. We don't just travel the world looking at bridges we are into whatever takes our fancy.

Mary Like making films?

Victoria Precisely. (*Getting a card from her handbag*) Here's my card. (*She hands it to Mary*) Have a think about it and give me a ring in a few days once I've talked to the ladies.

Malcolm Fine that's everyone fixed up except me.

Mary Only you can help yourself.

Roddy Keep telling him to get off his backside, but will he listen.

Malcolm I'm not doing it with you around that's for sure.

Sam enters

Sam Right, change of plan. We're using you now.

Mary All of us?

Sam Yes.

Mary But I haven't been to costume or make-up.

Sam We thought it would be a rather surreal twist if you are wearing normal clothing.

Malcolm You're making this up as you go along.

Sam No, the director thinks it will be deeply symbolic.

Malcolm (*putting his book into his bag*) Bolic is the right word.

Sam (*saying whatever comes into her head*) The different period costumes will simultaneously interlace with time thus giving the audience an experience of being both here and there at the same time.

Victoria Oh, I see.

Sam (*shocked*) You do!

Victoria Perfectly. (*She gets up and sorts out her handbag*)

Sam Good.

Roddy Why are we suddenly needed?

Sam Dirk's hurt himself, he needs a rest.

Roddy (*packing away his magazine*) Mirror fall on him?

Sam No, he fell of the climbing frame. My fault really. Well, yours to be precise. I accused him of having an affair with Howard.

Roddy So I was right!

Sam And he fell off laughing until he hit the ground. Then he categorically denied he was a bicycle. Why would I call him a bicycle?

Malcolm (*getting up*) Perhaps he said bisexual.

Sam Oh.

Roddy Does all this mean he's not having an affair with Howard?

Sam The only person he's having an affair with is himself. He's not bisexual he's monosexual.

Malcolm Don't you mean a monocycle.

Roddy But I caught him speaking to Howard.

Sam He says he's never spoken to Howard.

Roddy That's a lie I caught him on the phone to Howard the other day. When I pressed one-four-seven-one Dirk answered.

Sam Was that Wednesday evening?

Roddy Yes.

Sam That was me phoning Howard. I asked him if he knew anything about who was replacing the floor manager on his show. I hoped he could put in a good word for me.

Roddy And you share a flat with Dirk.

Sam He's been staying in my flat but those days are numbered. Ever since he landed this role he's gone further up himself than I thought was possible.

Victoria Don't worry he'll get his comeupperance.

Sam Anyway can't hang around gossiping. Are we all ready?

Sam exits followed by Malcolm and Mary

Victoria Oh yes I'm ready. (*Going up to Roddy*) I don't know about you but I can't wait to get my focus pulled.

As Victoria exits Roddy looks at her is disbelief, shakes his head, and then follows as ——

—— *the* CURTAIN *falls*

FURNITURE AND PROPERTY LIST

On stage: Large table. *On it*: mugs of tea, newspapers
Several chairs
Small table UR. *On it*: cooked breakfast, cutlery
2 chairs. *By one*: supermarket carrier bag containing a paperback (for **Malcolm**)
Smaller table UL. *On it*: bottle of tomato ketchup
2 chairs
Children's toys scattered on the floor UR
Children's paintings on L wall
Notice-board on R wall. *On it*: church notices and local event displays

Off stage: Piece of paper, handbag (**Mary**)
Tray containing cooked breakfast including sausage, holdall containing vitamin pills, bottled water, glass, cleaning equipment, camping magazine (**Roddy**)
Clipboard with forms, pen (**Sam**)
Large handbag containing expensive pen and notebook, cards (**Victoria**)
2 cups of coffee (**Victoria**)

Personal: **Sam**: headset

LIGHTING PLOT

Interior. The same scene throughout

To open: Full general lighting

No cues

EFFECTS PLOT

No cues

Lightning Source UK Ltd.
Milton Keynes UK
UKHW021532080522
402613UK00007B/370